I's
of
Autism

NAUGHTY'A GRAY

ISBN 978-1-0980-8570-4 (paperback)
ISBN 978-1-0980-8571-1 (digital)

Christian Faith Publishing, Inc.
832 Park Avenue
Meadville, PA 16335
www.christianfaithpublishing.com

Printed in the United States of America

To my nephew Cayden.

You are loved more than you know. You are smarter than you think. You are resilient in every sense of the word. Continue to be you and let your little light shine for the world to see.

Acknowledgment

Thanks to all who have supported the vision and mission for this book. You have made this opportunity a possibility. Thank you to my family for always supporting my dreams. Thank you to my friends for always lending an ear to hear my ideas. A big thank-you goes to Jesus Christ for speaking this book into my spirit. He is the true author of this book. We love because He first loved us (1 John 4:19).

Preface

Through the eyes of children, we see life in a beautiful and magical way. *I's of Autism* was divinely created to highlight the exceptionality of children with autism. It will encourage and empower the children, families, and anyone who reads the book. Although it may have an intended audience, I hope it opens the eyes of the world.

These children are amazing human beings created by a God who unconditionally loves us all. Remember this the next time a child with autism doesn't look you in the eyes. We are all children of God.

This book is inspired by God and has a biblical foundation. The dove on the cover represents hope of glory. The children are our gifts from God. Cherish them.

Oh, that I had the wings of a dove! I would fly away and be at rest. (Psalm 55:6)

When all the people were being baptized, Jesus was baptized too. And as he was praying, heaven was opened and the Holy Spirit descended on him in bodily form like a dove. And a voice came from heaven: "You are my Son, whom I love; with you I am well pleased." (Luke 3:21–22)

He called a little child to him, and placed the child among them. And he said: "Truly I tell you, unless you change and become like little children, you will never enter the kingdom of heaven. Therefore, whoever takes the lowly position of this child is the greatest in the kingdom of heaven." (Matthew 18:2–4)

Children are a heritage from the LORD, offspring a reward from him. (Psalm 127:3)

The eyes are a window to the soul.

—William Shakespeare

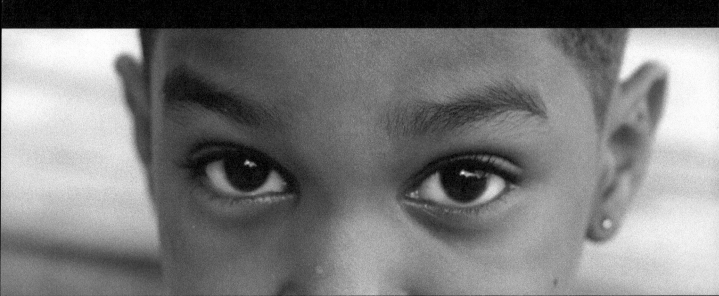

I am resilient.

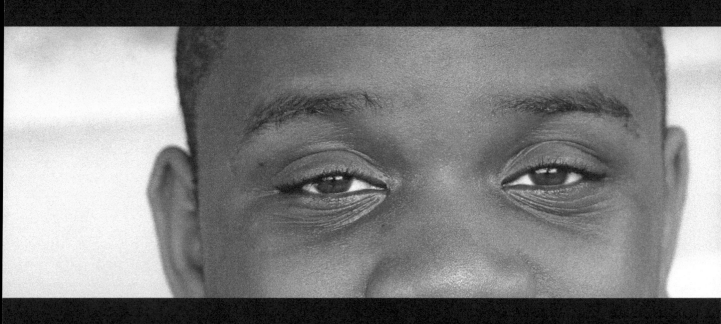

I am powerful.

I am strong.

I am smart.

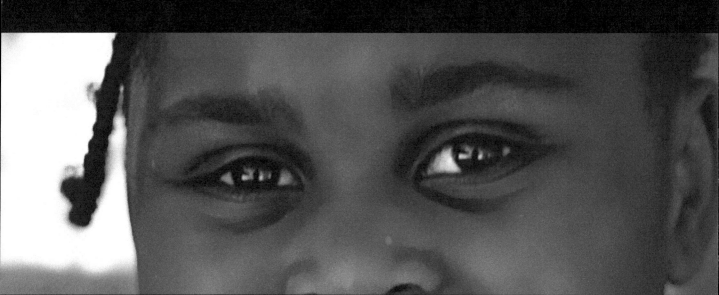

I am beautiful.

I am caring.

I am literal.

I am a child of God.

I am a son.

I am a daughter.

I am loved.

I am special.

I am talented.

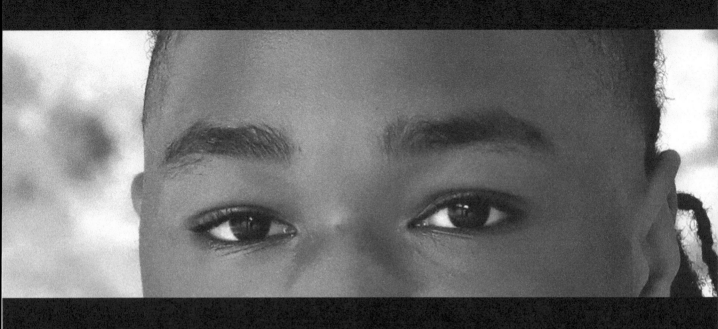

I am courageous.

I am me.

I am represented.

I am autistic.

The End

ABOUT THE AUTHOR

Naughty'a Gray is a mother, wife, educator, and entrepreneur. She graduated from Washington Adventist University in 2015 and has a bachelor's degree in Early Childhood Education and Care. She also attended Howard University and studied Human Development and Early Childhood Education. She is currently pursuing a master's degree in Leadership in Teaching. She loves to teach! Teaching is her passion and calling! She believes in being a life-long learner.

She has over fourteen years of childcare and teaching experience. She has been a tutor, babysitter, camp counselor, one-on-one paraprofessional, childcare teacher, a childcare center director, and a Head Start instructor. She has experience working with children ages birth to thirteen years and experience working in the special education field.

She was born in New York and grew up in Calvert County, Maryland. She loves the outdoors and adventure. She is a country girl at heart. Her favorite place to go and relax is the beach. She loves to travel and meet new people. She also enjoys shopping and spending time with her family. Her family is the most important thing to her.